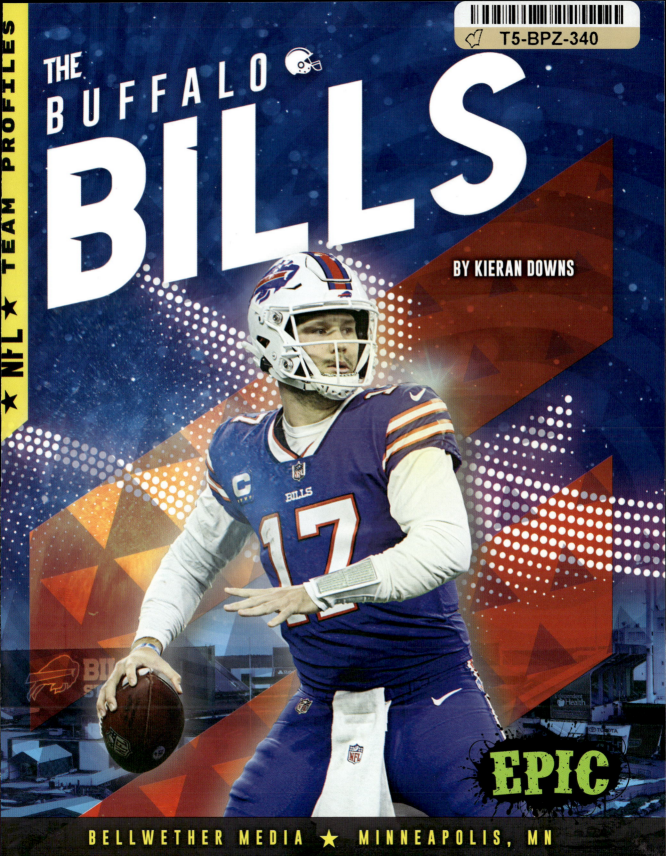

★ NFL ★ TEAM PROFILES

THE BUFFALO BILLS

BY KIERAN DOWNS

EPIC

BELLWETHER MEDIA ★ MINNEAPOLIS, MN

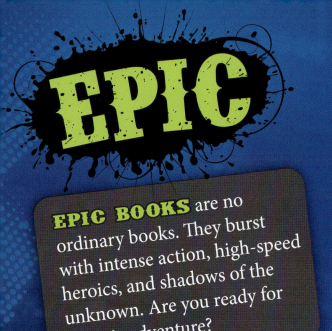

EPIC BOOKS are no ordinary books. They burst with intense action, high-speed heroics, and shadows of the unknown. Are you ready for an Epic adventure?

This edition first published in 2024 by Bellwether Media, Inc.

Library of Congress Cataloging-in-Publication Data

Names: Downs, Kieran, author.
Title: The Buffalo Bills / by Kieran Downs.
Description: Minneapolis, MN : Bellwether Media, 2024. | Series: Epic. NFL team profiles | Includes bibliographical references and index. | Audience: Ages 7-12 | Audience: Grades 2-3 | Summary: "Engaging images accompany information about the Buffalo Bills. The combination of high-interest subject matter and light text is intended for students in grades 2 through 7"--Provided by publisher.
Identifiers: LCCN 2023021283 (print) | LCCN 2023021284 (ebook) | ISBN 9798886874693 (library binding) | ISBN 9798886876574 (ebook)
Subjects: LCSH: Buffalo Bills (Football team)--History--Juvenile literature.
Classification: LCC GV956.B83 D68 2024 (print) | LCC GV956.B83 (ebook) | DDC 796.332/640974797--dc23/eng/20230508
LC record available at https://lccn.loc.gov/2023021283
LC ebook record available at https://lccn.loc.gov/2023021284

Editor: Betsy Rathburn   Designer: Gabriel Hilger

Printed in the United States of America, North Mankato, MN.

TABLE OF CONTENTS

A BIG WIN

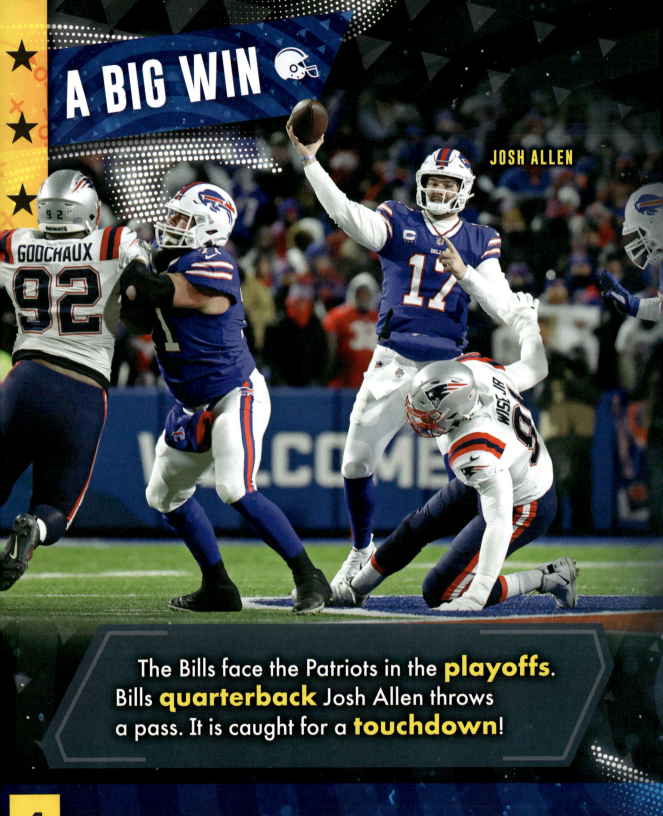

JOSH ALLEN

The Bills face the Patriots in the **playoffs**. Bills **quarterback** Josh Allen throws a pass. It is caught for a **touchdown**!

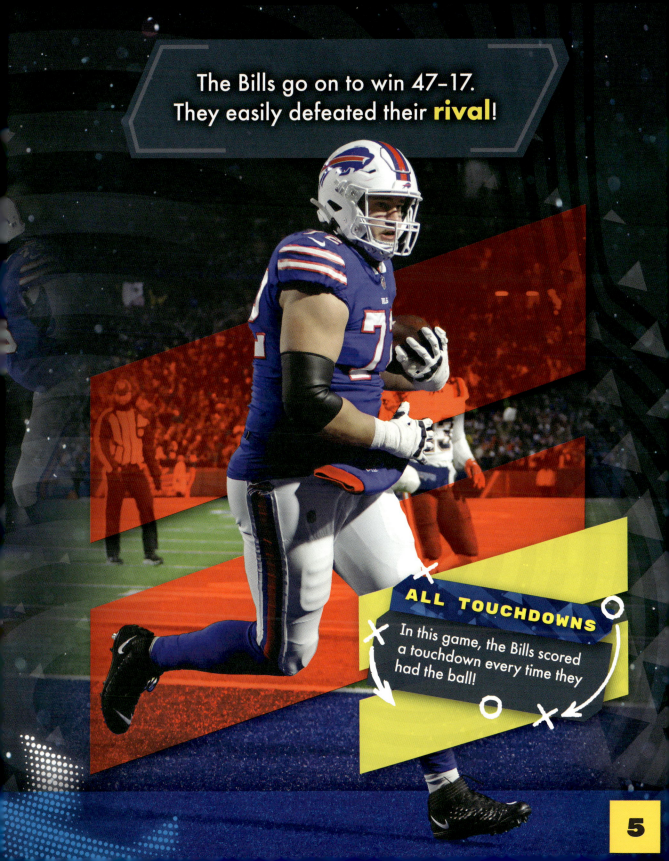

The Bills go on to win 47–17. They easily defeated their **rival**!

ALL TOUCHDOWNS

In this game, the Bills scored a touchdown every time they had the ball!

THE HISTORY OF THE BILLS

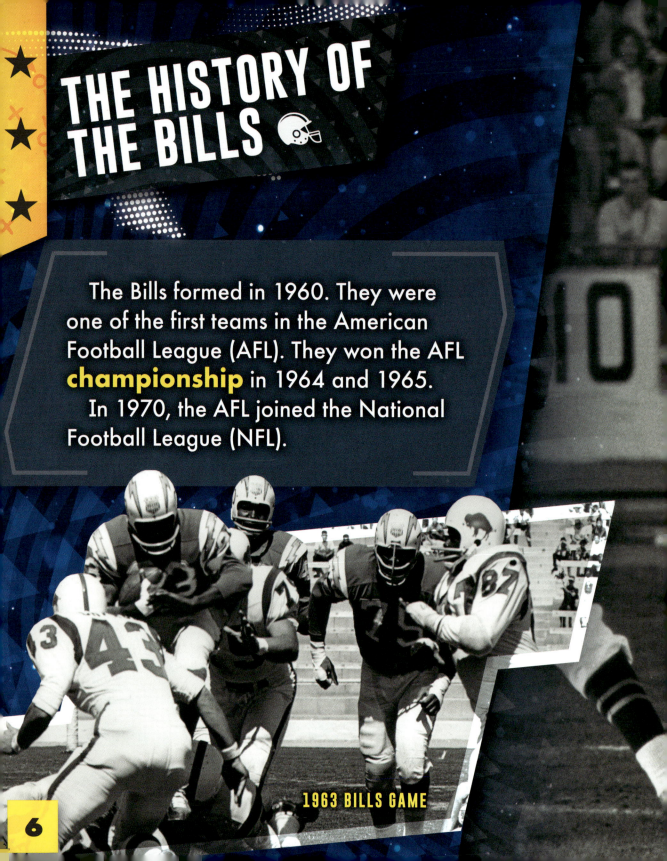

The Bills formed in 1960. They were one of the first teams in the American Football League (AFL). They won the AFL **championship** in 1964 and 1965. In 1970, the AFL joined the National Football League (NFL).

1963 BILLS GAME

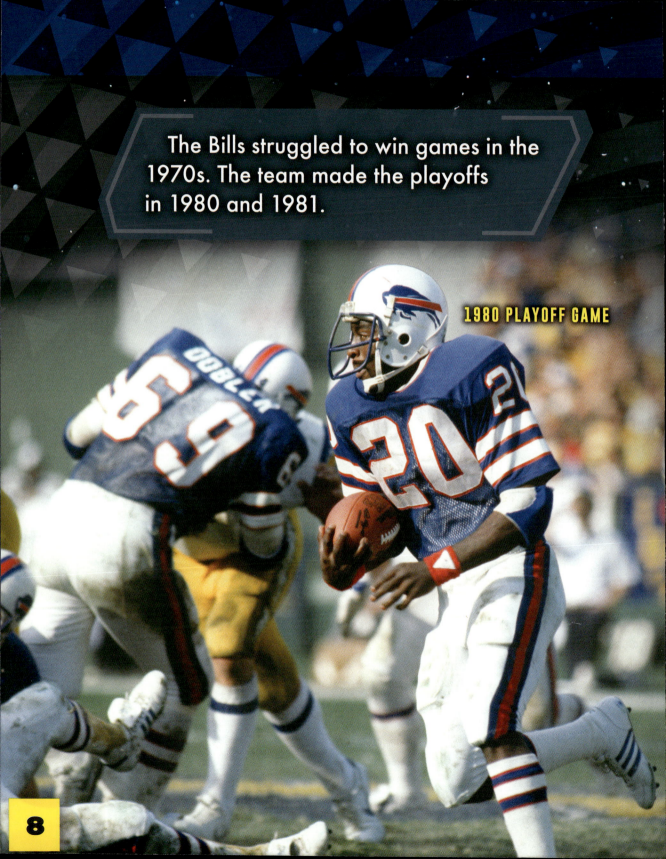

The Bills struggled to win games in the 1970s. The team made the playoffs in 1980 and 1981.

1980 PLAYOFF GAME

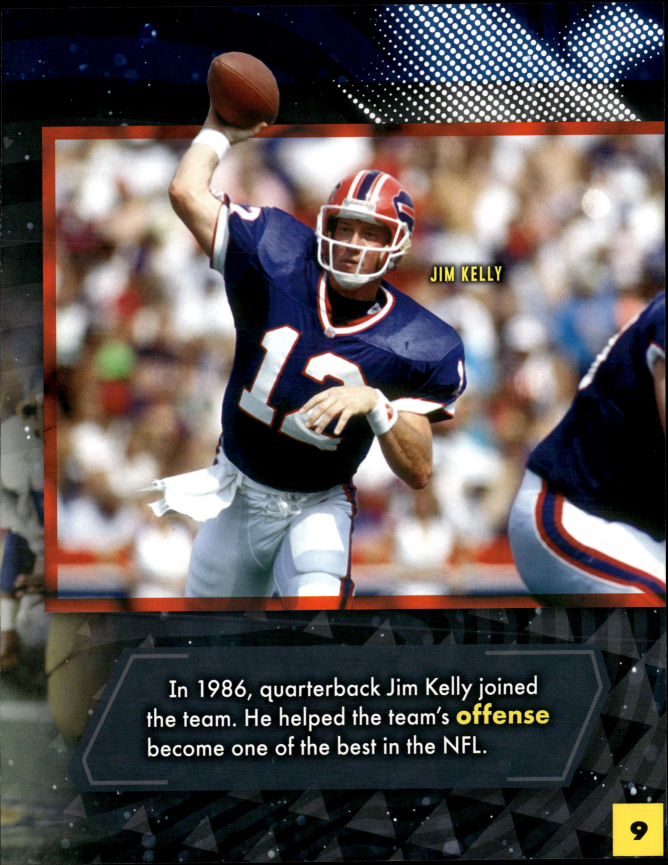

JIM KELLY

In 1986, quarterback Jim Kelly joined the team. He helped the team's **offense** become one of the best in the NFL.

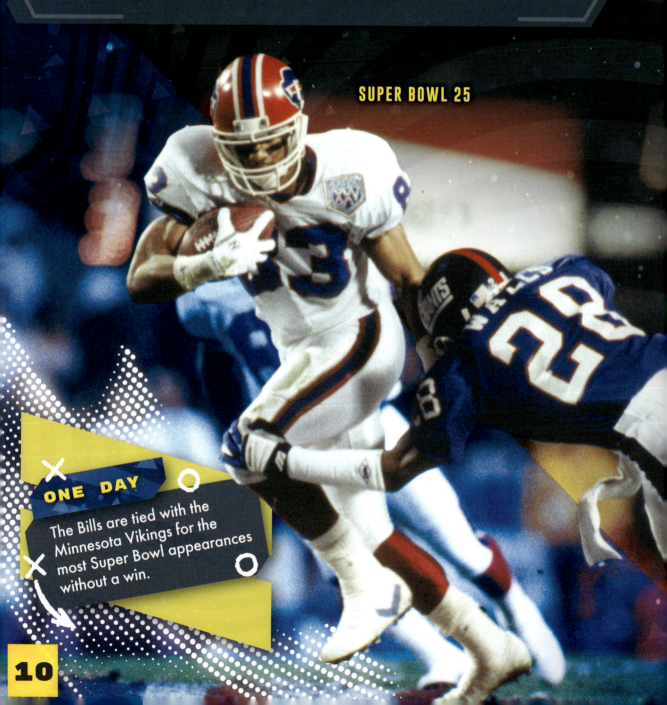

In 1991, the Bills played in their first **Super Bowl**. But they lost to the New York Giants.

SUPER BOWL 25

ONE DAY

The Bills are tied with the Minnesota Vikings for the most Super Bowl appearances without a win.

The Bills made the Super Bowl every year for the next three years. But they lost all of them.

🏆 TROPHY CASE 🏆

SUPER BOWL appearances
4

AFC EAST championships
10

PLAYOFF appearances
22

AFL championships
2

The Bills struggled again in the 2000s. They did not make the playoffs from 2000 to 2017.

2014 BILLS GAME

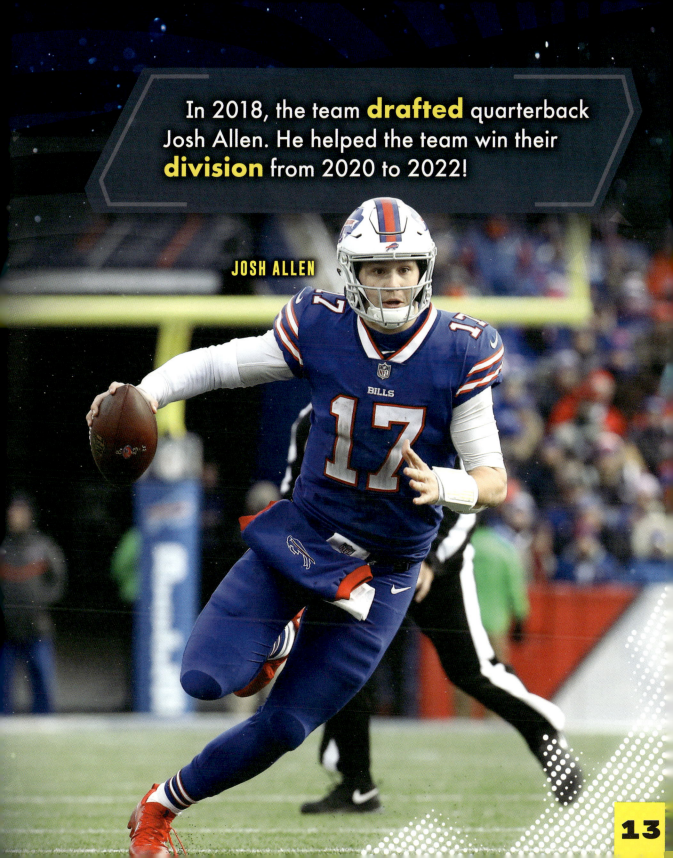

In 2018, the team **drafted** quarterback Josh Allen. He helped the team win their **division** from 2020 to 2022!

JOSH ALLEN

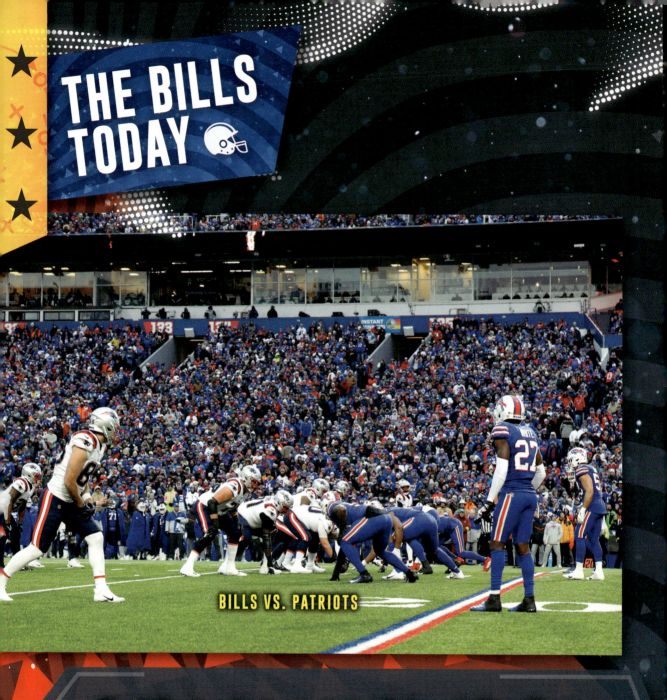

THE BILLS TODAY

BILLS VS. PATRIOTS

The Bills play their games in Highmark **Stadium**. It is in Orchard Park, New York.

The team plays in the AFC East division. Their biggest rivals are the Miami Dolphins and the New England Patriots.

LOCATION

NEW YORK

HIGHMARK STADIUM

Orchard Park, New York

N
W E
S

GAME DAY!

Bills fans like to party before home games. Many enjoy **tailgating**.

They cook food and play games in the stadium's parking lot. Buffalo chicken wings are a favorite tailgate food.

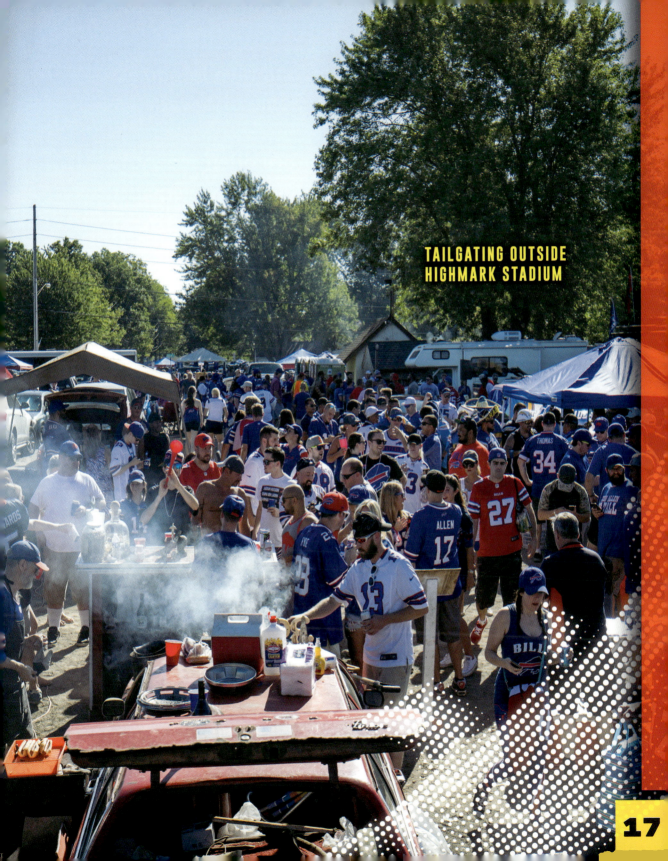

TAILGATING OUTSIDE HIGHMARK STADIUM

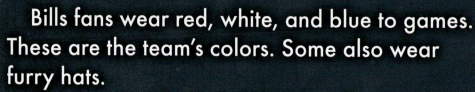

Bills fans wear red, white, and blue to games. These are the team's colors. Some also wear furry hats.

Home games in the winter are often snowy. But Bills fans cheer for the team in any weather!

SNOW BOWL

SNOW BOWL

On December 10, 2017, it snowed around 9 inches (23 centimeters) during the Bills game. The Bills beat the Indianapolis Colts 13–7.

★ FAMOUS PLAYERS ★

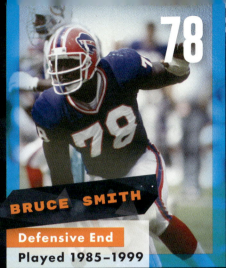

78

BRUCE SMITH
Defensive End
Played 1985–1999

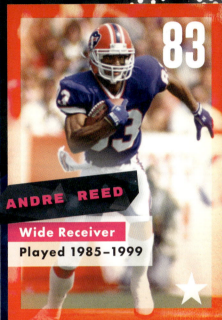

83

ANDRE REED
Wide Receiver
Played 1985–1999

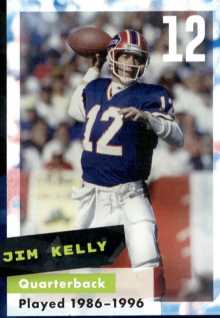

12

JIM KELLY
Quarterback
Played 1986–1996

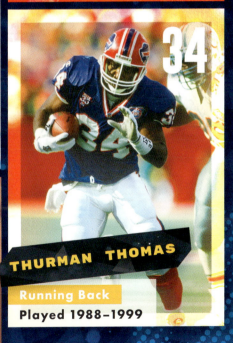

34

THURMAN THOMAS
Running Back
Played 1988–1999

17

JOSH ALLEN
Quarterback
Played 2018–present

BUFFALO BILLS FACTS

LOGO

JOINED THE NFL	**1970** (AFL 1960–1969)
NICKNAMES	None

MASCOT

BILLY BUFFALO

CONFERENCE

American Football Conference (AFC)

COLORS

DIVISION	AFC East

Miami Dolphins

New England Patriots

New York Jets

STADIUM

★ HIGHMARK STADIUM ★

opened August 17, 1973

holds **71,608** people

⏱ TIMELINE

1960
The Buffalo Bills form

1964
The Bills win their first AFL Championship Game

1991
The Bills play in their first Super Bowl

2017
The Bills make the playoffs for the first time in 18 years

2020
The Bills win their division for the first time since 1995

★ RECORDS ★

All-Time Passing Leader	All-Time Rushing Leader	All-Time Receiving Leader	All-Time Scoring Leader

Jim Kelly
35,467 yards

Thurman Thomas
11,938 yards

Andre Reed
13,095 yards

Steve Christie
1,011 points

21

GLOSSARY

championship—a contest to decide the best team or person

division—a group of NFL teams from the same area that often play against each other; there are eight divisions in the NFL.

drafted—chose a college athlete to play for a professional team

offense—the group of players who have the ball and try to score

playoffs—games played after the regular season is over; playoff games determine which teams play in the championship game.

quarterback—a player whose main job is to throw and hand off the ball

rival—a long-standing opponent

stadium—an arena where sports are played

Super Bowl—the annual championship game of the NFL

tailgating—having a party in the parking lot at a sporting event

touchdown—a score that occurs when a team crosses into their opponent's end zone with the football; a touchdown is worth six points.

TO LEARN MORE

AT THE LIBRARY

Abdo, Kenny. *Buffalo Bills*. Minneapolis, Minn.: Abdo Zoom, 2022.

Coleman, Ted. *Buffalo Bills*. Mendota Heights, Minn.: Press Room Editions, 2022.

Pettiford, Rebecca. *Josh Allen*. Minneapolis, Minn.: Bellwether Media, 2024.

ON THE WEB

FACTSURFER

Factsurfer.com gives you a safe, fun way to find more information.

1. Go to www.factsurfer.com.

2. Enter "Buffalo Bills" into the search box and click Q.

3. Select your book cover to see a list of related content.

INDEX